# Creatives' homes

TAVERNE AGENCY

TERRA

## THE AUTHORS

As the founder of Taverne Agency, **Nathalie Taverne** has spent the past eleven years working with the world's finest interior, lifestyle and food photographers, ensuring their work appears in the world's finest magazines. Within the Taverne collection, original and inspirational homes from around the world are brought together under one roof, with the stories of those who design and live in them as fascinating as the photographs are beautiful. Nathalie and her husband and business partner Robert Borghuis live and work in Amsterdam and together find time to raise their two children, Elena and John.

Having begun her writing career on the *Financial Times'* award-winning *How To Spend It* magazine, **Anna Lambert** went on to spend three years working in the Netherlands, where she met and started working with Nathalie Taverne. Anna's work has appeared in interiors magazines worldwide, including *Australian Vogue Living, World of Interiors, Elle Decoration* and *Elle Wonen*, and she is the author of *Easy Living, Inspirational Apartments* and, with Nathalie Taverne, of *The Natural Home, Vintage Living* and *Small Homes*, all published by Terra Lannoo. She lives with her husband and two daughters in the UK.

© 2011 Uitgeverij Terra Lannoo B.V.
P.O. Box 614, 6800 AP Arnhem
The Netherlands
info@terralannoo.nl
www.terralannoo.nl
Uitgeverij Terra is part of the Lannoo group, Belgium

Text and images: © 2011 Taverne Agency B.V.
Lisdoddelaan 79
1087 KB Amsterdam
The Netherlands
www.taverneagency.com

Compilation: Nathalie Taverne
Text: Anna Lambert
Design: Ben Lambers, Studio Aandacht
Printed and bound: Leo Paper Products Ltd., Hongkong

ISBN 978 90 8989 283 6
NUR 454
Also published in Dutch as *Huizen van creatives*
(ISBN 978 90 8989 282 9)

# We are all creatives within our own four walls

We are, of course, all creatives when it comes to our own homes, because that's what having your own space is all about: making it work for you and your family, putting your stamp on it. But those working in the creative professions may have a different approach – for a start, many of them are likely to actually work within their domestic settings, rather than merely living there.

Then there's the way in which they approach the decoration of their homes – are they practical when it comes to the day-to-day business of living in their homes, or do they tend to regard their spaces as domestic galleries, testaments to their own skills and passions? Or perhaps – preoccupied as they may be with work throughout the day – they may prefer to design their homes as restful spaces, possibly devoid of colour or extraneous detail.

Over the following pages, we'll see all sorts of inspirational approaches represented, and by everyone from artists in Brazil to photographers on Ibiza. What unifies all these homes is the commitment that their various owners have given to them, and the joy and sense of security that they, in return, clearly give to their creative owners.

# At one with wood

**This simple studio, belonging to craftsman Andrea Brugi and situated in the backstreets of the ancient and beautiful Italian village of Montemerano, shows how it's possible to turn a working environment into a 'home from home'. It's here that Andrea designs and makes his simple, rustic-style wooden pieces – everything from pots to furniture – in a pared-down setting that he finds inspirational.**

Getting back to nature is something that creative people will always find invigorating, and in his studio, Andrea Brugi can't complain that he's not surrounded by its fruits. Not only is his *laboratorio* brimming with completed pieces of his woodwork designs – ranging from tiny containers for salt and pepper, wooden serving platters and roughly-hewn, lovingly-finished chopping boards to tables, benches and hanging rails – you'll also find reclaimed wood just waiting to be reinvented. While some of it takes the form of discarded doors, chairs missing a leg or two, old railway sleepers, fences, gates and window shutters, there's wood in its original state, too.

Roots from the local olive trees, for instance, which can be up to four centuries old, trunks and branches from local chestnut and elm trees, even an actual olive tree, which, growing straight through the floor, helps to breathe continued life into this old place.

# Trees breathe continued life into this old place

For Andrea, even the humblest of objects can prove inspirational. He has been collecting vintage tools since boyhood, responding to the warmth of their old wooden handles, the faded patina of their steel. And, grouped together and wall-mounted, they do appear as some sort of artisanal art installation. But, of course, this isn't just about an aesthetic approach – it's a wholly practical one, too: many of these old chisels, lathes and gimlets allow for an individuality of finish that their modern successors simply can't offer.

Just as Andrea Brugi tells people that the designs of his pieces are dictated by the wood itself, so this space is dictated by the materials used in its creation – the crumbling plasterwork and ancient beams provide the ideal working environment for someone who thrives on objects that bear the marks of age and usage. While this can never be a space that's ideal for the practicalities of 21st-century living, it is one that feeds its inhabitant's creativity. In a similar way, each of Andrea's wooden chopping boards is 'fed' with olive oil from the Brugi family's farm, with the oil keeping the pieces supple and nourished and helping them to 'self-clean'. It seems an appropriate living metaphor for the relationship between one man and his materials, and those materials and their setting.

# Into the white

**On the island of Ibiza, this once-abandoned finca has been transformed into the most calm-inducing of spaces by an artist and her photographer partner, who use it as both home and atelier. Though the farmhouse retains all the integrity of its original design, the couple have imbued it with a contemporary energy that's all their own.**

This all-white, light-filled farmhouse, with its stone and concrete floors, exposed brickwork and bleached rafters, serves as the ideal backdrop to the lives and work of its owners. The artist Linde Bialas uses what was once a farmer's carpentry workshop as her studio, creating a sense of continuity: just as the original occupants worked in here to create things with wood, Linde creates large-scale works that she has exhibited throughout Europe. Meanwhile, her photographer husband, Chico Bialas, has also taken the house and its setting as his inspiration – not only are the rooms of his home enlivened by his photographic portraits, but Ibiza itself has proved the catalyst for his book, *Ibiza: A Passion.*

# White-painted walls allow light to bounce around the space

Throughout the finca, the white-chalk-painted walls allow light to bounce around the space, while a mixture of treasures means there's something of interest in every room. In the kitchen, for instance, the worktop is covered with old faience tiles found in antique shops on the island, while the blackboard is covered in Arabic writing and bears the legend, 'Room for rent'. In the main living room, a Moroccan rug adds a splash of colour. Meanwhile, photographic portraits by Chico add mood to the various areas, and one wall is punctuated by a hanging sculpture created by the couple's son, Martin. What furniture there is in this home has been carefully chosen, with pieces by Mies van der Rohe, Charles and Ray Eames and Poul Kjaerholm. Added to the mix are lamps picked up in flea markets and the odd French chair from the 1940s, plus an antique wooden table and original Tolix chairs in the dining room. There's even an old rubber-glove mould on display – which makes a surprisingly effective sculpture when placed in one of the finca's many alcoves. This, then, is truly a home that both shelters and nurtures its occupants, allowing them a space in which they can unwind and recharge their batteries before going on to apply their restored energies to creating more art. The Bialas' finca serves not just a practical purpose, but a highly personal, inspirational one, too.

# A polymath's home

**This home in the Florentine countryside has been created from top to bottom by its polymath owner, artist Gianni Neri. Not only did he carry out the conversion and refurbishment of what was once an old hay barn himself, he has also filled it with his own diverse range of creations, ranging from interior design to paintings and sculptures. And his talents are not confined to the visual arts – he's a musician, too. Hardly surprising, then, that this is a house filled with colour, warmth, art and music.**

For Gianni Neri, this house is not only a home, but a series of canvases, too. It seems he's regarded every space as a potential mini artwork: using cement creatively, for instance, on the house's floors and masonry, and lime-washing its walls in rich shades from ochre to terracotta, grey to teal blue. Meanwhile, in those areas on the first floor of the house in which he tends to think and meditate, a neutral backdrop of calm white tones has been introduced. Gianni speaks of his "...need to create without succumbing to the power of technology or the lure of mass-market production", and everywhere are signs both of that creativity and the extraordinary, one-off diversity of his skills. In the bathroom, for instance, you'll find not only a cement basin that he made himself, but one of his elongated plaster sculptures, too. In the kitchen, it's the stripes of the lime wash that dominate this masculine space, accentuated by the

warm grey of the cement-hewn work surfaces and the combination of an old marble-topped table with paint-splattered stools. Understandably, Gianni's use of colour is less heavy in his bedroom, with its white-washed floors and walls. Only an ochre-tinted area provides fixed colour; in the rest of the space, it is introduced via accessories such as the linen throw on the bed, hand-painted by artist Lietta Cavalli. Gianni made the bed and tables here himself, painting them with a silvery, light-reflecting finish that brings a subtle sparkle to the room.

Elsewhere, it seems, Gianni shares the house with the extraordinary small wire figures suspended from the ceiling in his studio. It's not just sculpture that's produced here, though – everything from jewellery to video installations emerge from this space.

This home is about all aspects of the creative process – about making things, living with them, enjoying them. But, like its owner, it's impossible to categorise. It is full of colours and textures – from the rough feel of linen to the cool finish of cement and marble – while the art here embraces every possible medium, from paint and clay to glass, wood and wire. As such, it's an invigorating, ever-changing space that succeeds in providing constant inspiration for its equally energetic owner.

# an't be easily categorised

# The collector

You might imagine that a person who is surrounded by top design products at work all day would want to come home to a relatively pared-down environment. Not John Parker, Melbourne-based manager of the Space Furniture store. His home, converted from what was once an army marching hall, is an airy, light-filled showcase for his personal collection of colourful art and the very best of contemporary home accessories.

John Parker's packed Melbourne home works because its owner has one guiding principle when it comes to choosing items. "I'm passionate about great design, and everything here is something I really love," he says simply. His industrial-feel, split-level apartment boasts pieces by Melbourne artists such as Judy Singleton, Dean Bowen and David Larwill, most of whom he knows personally and first befriended when they were struggling unknowns. But his home doesn't just make a feature out of the art and accessories he loves – he celebrates the utilitarian too: his bike collection, for instance, is on view, while clothes hang suspended via an Edra clothing rail, like some sort of sculptural display. It helps that many of the garments are in the bright primary colours that punctuate

# If I see something love at work, I just have to have it at home, too

his home decor elsewhere: yellow in the kitchen, as seen on a feature wall, and blue and red via the mobiles that hang down in the living area. Just as John Parker doesn't like to restrict his view of what constitutes art, he also doesn't like to restrict how he lives. Maybe that's one reason that he doesn't have a bedroom, as such, within the space – instead, he prefers to take his sleeping kit from room to room, often bedding down on the upper deck in summer and in his office area in winter. He is, perhaps thankfully, just slightly more conventional when it comes to bathroom arrangements, with a loo and shower housed in an opaque glass box off his dressing area.

In the kitchen, too, he takes a practical approach, opting for utilitarian, moveable pieces designed by the likes of Kartell and Arc Linea, together with a Less kitchen table, designed by Jean Nouvel for Unifor.

As far as furniture elsewhere is concerned, pieces John Parker couldn't resist include a Sciangai wig-wam-like clothes rack by Zanotta, Edra's Flap sofa in the living area, and the Campana brothers' Favela chairs, which provide an ideal counter-point to the old army battalion mascot (a nod to the fact that this was once a marching hall). "If I see something at Space that I love, it isn't enough just to be able to admire it there – I have to have it at home, too," he confesses. "I guess that's how I've managed to end up with so much stuff..." These are surely words to which anyone who has found themselves compelled to go that step beyond mere window shopping can well relate! John Parker's home proves that high style and practicality can live side by side – providing, that is, you're prepared to incorporate bikes, clothes and lack of a bed into everyday living. It works for him, and surely that's the only thing that matters.

# Living
# gallery

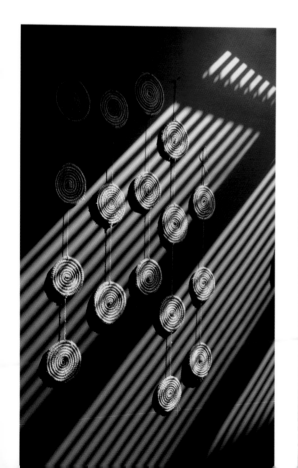

This award-winning Sydney warehouse conversion is the home of property developer and designer, Linda Gregoriou.
In its design, she has created a calming, restful space that provides the perfect foil to her vibrant collection of art. Moreover, with its simple white-washed, sun-kissed walls and central water-filled courtyard, she says it has echoes of the Greek-Cypriot homes that she grew up with.

Different creative types thrive in different sorts of settings, and Linda Gregoriou is someone whose ideal setting is a retreat-like space. Her home surprises many first-time visitors, who are amazed that somewhere so restful and enclosed can be found right in the heart of the city. The building itself, which runs over three levels, was converted by architect Graham Jahn, and perhaps its most striking feature – beyond the general sense of light and space – is the little courtyard complete with water and stepping-stones. Utilising a naturally-occurring stream running under the warehouse, it's a contemplative space, reminiscent of a Japanese water garden. With the conversion incorporating key features such as plenty of concrete, cement flooring and an aluminium-alloy feature wall, it could – in the wrong hands – have ended up with an inappropriately sterile feel. Indoors, though, Linda has brought visual warmth to the place, first and foremost via her outstanding collection of aboriginal art, which she began collecting over fifteen years ago. She has grouped works by colour so that they form a rich, lively tableau, and in shades ranging from reds, oranges and corals to rosy pinks ("My lipstick wall", as Linda refers to this area of her collection), soft browns and ochres. Accessories, too, enliven the space, with Iranian silk rugs in the living room, and Ingo Maurer's Zettel lamp hanging over the dining area. There's also furniture from China (a lacquered dining table plus antique Oxbow chairs, for instance), as well as the simplest of vessels and an antique, hand-painted screen, separating the kitchen from the dining area, all from Japan. Raffia baskets, from Maningrida in northern Australia, make striking pieces in their own right when wall-mounted, while rattan fish traps take on a sculptural quality in the living room. Elsewhere, Linda's family of little woven Bush dollies, each one a different character, have a whimsical charm.

Linda's home is a testament to one woman's passion for, interest in and commitment to the art and culture of her Australian homeland. It's an absorbing space, in which there's always something new to experience and enjoy, while, at the same time, the restful air it exudes means it's also somewhere truly rejuvenating.

# Quirky pieces add charm

# A vast expanse of wall provide the perfect setting for these vibrant artworks

# Cottage style

**In his tiny period cottage ("It was described as 'a doll's house', so I never expected to end up in it – but here I am. I think it has worked in practical terms because my studio's elsewhere..."), Melbourne-based artist Thornton Walker combines unexpected colours with the plainest of furnishings and accessories. Coupled with the warmth of internal wood cladding, the result is a rich, simple and beautiful home.**

It's reassuring to be reminded that creatives can be every bit as practical in their approach to home-owning as their more prosaically-employed counterparts. When viewing this little cottage for the first time, artist Thornton Walker was concerned that it would be too small to suit his needs, but, having fallen for it, he has ensured it has ended up working well for him. For a start, he extended the space by adding a kitchen and a bathroom. The situation is also helped by the fact that his primary studio – roughly the size of this house again – is located in another part of Melbourne. Hence, this cottage serves mainly as a domestic space, with a studio area that's been kept deliberately small so it doesn't dominate. He has also stripped out any of the extraneous decorative detail that he inherited from previous owners,

including highly-patterned wallpaper. In its place is rough-hewn plaster, which provides an ideal textural counterpoint to the wood cladding that dominates – not just on the walls, but through its use in Walker's designs for the kitchen furniture, too. This lends the cottage so much detail in itself that he has been able to keep everything else simple, from the shapes of his sofas to his wooden, open-plan shelving in the kitchen and the original pigeon-holes that he uses to display a collection of old china. Strong colour has been introduced via throws and cushions in hot red and a wall-mounted shield in the living room,

but the other shade that really stands out is the soft, almost verdigris, green that he has used on door and window frames, adding a cooling element to the mix. Window treatments show a similar commitment to the concept of keeping it simple – an old, plain sari at the bathroom window, for instance, provides low-key privacy.

As important to Walker as the house is his garden, a pretty little suntrap in which he can grow flowers and vegetables, then cook with the results. Clearly his is a world in which he's as happy to experiment with domestic creativity as he is with the artistic kind.

# Pale green cools things down

# A passion for stuff

In both his Victoria, Australia, home and his old warehouses, artist and retailer David Bromley reveals his passion for objects in all their rich diversity. Acquiring artefacts might be one of the ways in which he makes a very successful living, but, for him, it's more of a compulsion than a job.

Even by the standards of creative personalities, David Bromley has extraordinary reserves of energy. Not only is he an artist whose work is represented in both Australia and Britain, he also finds time to renovate sizeable properties (some thirty to date), to lease out space in his storage and studio facilities, and to renovate artefacts and furniture to sell in his shop, A Day On Earth. No wonder his house – once the home of influential mid-21st-century Australian artist Albert Tucker – in the St Kilda suburb of Melbourne has particular significance as a place in which he can re-energise, along with his wife, fashion designer Tori Dixon-Whittle, and their young family.

A bolt-hole it may be, but the house, which dates from 1868, bears all the hallmarks of Bromley's style in its eclecticism. Here, you'll find vintage treasures such as classic Eames recliners and Danish leather furniture jostling for attention next to apothecary jars, reclaimed pottery and art by unknown Eastern European artists. For Bromley, it seems, is a man who thrives when surrounded, not just by the familiar, but also by that which isn't so easily defined, identified or categorised. It makes living with objects so much more interesting.

Despite the mix of styles and periods within his home, Bromley's look works. While this is undoubtedly down to his sophisticated eye, it has helped, too, that this self-confessed hoarder, who appreciates nothing more than living with things for a while before selling them on, has plenty of additional space – including three vast cannery warehouses a couple of hours' drive from Melbourne – in which to store extraneous pieces. These might comprise anything from the magnificent 1950s' Borgward Isabella coupé he bought his wife for her birthday, to room sets that he has put together from pieces members of his team have extensively renovated and that he plans to sell on. When it comes to his 'day job' as an artist, meanwhile, Bromley is fortunate enough, too, to have a studio that's separate from his living space in St Kilda, located as it is in what were once the house's stables. What comes across in both David Bromley's living and working spaces is his genuine love for the objects that surround him and his interest in their prospects for reinvention. This isn't a man who acquires things simply because he makes a good living out of it, but, rather, because he's truly fascinated by the history of pieces – whether known or unknown. An artist himself, he's able to appreciate the work that has gone into them and the attachment that past owners may have had for them. As he has said in the past, "Yes, if I understand and know and like what I sell, then I have a greater chance of selling it. But I'm obsessed with arranging things in a space. It's my hobby and I love it."

# It's quite a mix – but it works

# Past, present, future

**Artist Tracey Tawhiao's New Zealand home, which she shares with her partner and their two daughters, couples her own brand of imagery with that of her traditional Maori heritage, with her decor being largely influenced by Maori Wharenui Ceremonial houses. "I've tried to take the philosophy and aesthetic – which emphasise the importance of ritual and creativity – into my own home," she says, – and the result is an intriguing, almost mystical, home.**

Words and symbols abound in the decor of Tracey Tawhiao's west-of-Auckland home – hardly surprising, given the symbolism that forms such an important part of her own Maori heritage, and her work as a poet whose verse is studied in New Zealand's university literature courses. If words can be incorporated into this home, they are; a simple glass door, for instance, is covered with words that have inspired Tracey or captured her imagination, fleeting thoughts and ideas. Elsewhere, the walls are covered with her own works, which incorporate ancient Maori symbols representing ancient elements and life forces. It's a highly evocative, spiritual mix, but Tracey's use of strong colour and the playful simplicity of her style mean her work is never overly self-reverential – rather, it's thought-provoking yet easy to live with.

# Here, Tracey has used a simple colour palette

Tracey's newspaper paintings are particularly celebrated: she'll use either acrylic paint or pastels on newspaper, painting freehand and playing with text and headlines to give the words a new meaning, as well as incorporating symbols from Maori culture. "My work has been called naïve," she has said, "because it's unmeasured and hand drawn – but there is a contrast between the naïve and the intellectual." Hung as wallpaper, the works succeed in being both decorative and challenging – Tracey has used them in her own dining room, where they contrast with a vintage 1950s' teak table and chairs.

It would be easy to imagine that a space like this, where so many surfaces are embellished – not just glass doors, but walls and windows too – might seem a little... well, 'noisy'. Far from it. Colour and light in Tracey Tawhiao's home are cleverly utilised to create a home that's both playful and relaxing. In the living room, for instance, which enjoys a magnificent view over the harbour, the palette has been restricted to simple, natural shades of whites and buffs, so that nothing detracts from the water beyond. Light bounces off that water and into the room, then darts around the white furniture and walls therein, to magical effect.

The light-filled atelier on the house's ground floor offers plenty of space in which Tracey can experiment, and its concrete surfaces are littered with work in progress – here, the greens and yellows pick up on the natural colours of the world beyond. By filling it with her art, Tracey Tawhiao has created a home that's about past recollections, history and celebration: "When you have been colonised, as the Maori people have," she has said in previous interviews, "you have to retain a personal memory of your culture within your everyday existence, and your home is one of the few places in which you're able to do that." What's particularly interesting is that she has succeeded in not making a space that's about nostalgia or sadness. Rather, in embracing the past and aspects of Maori culture through her use of symbolism, imagery, words and colour, she seems to have created a platform for herself and her family from which they're able to look to the future with clear-headed optimism.

# New from old

**In the mountains around Rio de Janeiro, artists Zemog and Rita Dias have created an extraordinary, colourful home in which almost everything demands to be touched. What's more, in their installations, artworks and sculptures, they've used recycled, reclaimed and organic materials wherever possible – either found on the street, donated by friends or bought cheaply in the marketplace. In their hands, old cotton T-shirts, battered tin cans and discarded bottle-tops take on an entirely new identity...**

It probably helps in this Brazilian home that co-owner Zemog Dias has something of an obsession with bottle-tops: "I have literally thousands of them – friends collect them for me, café owners donate them to me. I can't see one on the ground without stopping to pick it up..." Having acquired them, he flattens them, shapes them and arranges them by colour, stitching them onto artworks or threading them to produce sinuously coiled knot shapes, some seven metres long, that are then wall-mounted in the home he shares with his wife Rita. She, needless to say, has her own passions:

in her case, anything that glistens. Taking as its inspiration the traditional costumes of Mexico and Africa, and displayed in various rooms within the couple's gallery-cum-home, is Rita's jewellery, which sees glass combined with tiny wooden birds and animals.

Her own-design chandeliers – embellished with everything from corks to buttons as well as jewels – hang from the ceilings of their 19th-century Portuguese-style house. With numerous mirrors to reflect the light that they cast, it's no wonder that this house really does seem to sparkle.

The home itself is neo-classical in design

# In this home, more is more

and dates from 1876. Its period proportions – grand-scale rooms and high ceilings – make the modernity of the couple's pieces seem all the more striking. No surface here is undecorated.

There's nothing Zemog can't – or won't – turn his hand to: if other people are discarding chairs with ugly upholstery, he'll take them home and recover them. Tables and benches he has made from reclaimed wood have been enlivened by the addition of details such as wooden 'fringing', made from unwanted old spindles. Throwing out these empty olive-oil cans and that vast tin bucket? Zemog will refashion them into a quirky side-table instead. It's the creation of these wholly new pieces from old items that really excites him, and, four times a year, he and Rita open up their doors to exhibit their creations to visitors. In the living room hangs his series of works,

woven from reclaimed Catholic ribbons bearing saints' names, cheekily entitled 'Para combinar com o sofa' ('To match the sofa'). Arranged by size and colour, the pieces make an eye-catching collection that undoubtedly do pick up on the tones and colours used elsewhere in the room. This couple like to put their stamp on everything – Rita has jazzed up the table and chairs in the dining area, for instance, by adding a few white spots, while Zemog was not content with just creating a bottle-top-fringed curtain for the kitchen, he felt the need to add a few faux pearls, too...

With such energy and enthusiasm displayed by its owners – and such lively, innovative pieces on display on the walls – it's hardly surprising that this house provides a truly invigorating setting, not just for those who live in it, but for those who visit it, too.

# There's not a
# blank surface
# in sight

# Mixing business with pleasure

**International photographer Urko Suaya's Buenos Aires home-cum-studio – a converted loft that was originally a carpenter's workshop – works so well for him precisely because he sees his work as being inseparable from his personality.
"Photography isn't just my job – it's who I am," he says.**

The owners' initial response to this space has dictated its use. When Urko Suaya and his sculptress wife Celina Saubidet first saw it, their intention was to use the front half of the building to live in, and to use the vast space beyond the courtyard garden as Urko's photographic studio. He's a highly successful photographer whose work has appeared in fashion magazines around the world, so the couple knew they'd need a decent-sized space for Urko to work in. Eventually, though, they decided that what was on offer was too good to be kept solely for business. Instead, they commissioned local architect Isabelle Firmin-Didot to devise

a second storey for the property, and – because of the size of the space they had to fill – to create furniture specifically for it, including bookshelves, tables and beds. Today, while the upstairs houses a living room, bedroom, kitchen and bathroom, downstairs features the studio space, for which the furniture comes complete with castors. This means that the monolithic dining table and benches, for instance, can be wheeled out of the way when Urko needs to clear the space for photo shoots. The front part of the building, meanwhile, is given over to an office and meeting space as well as make-up studio and eating area.

Maximising the sense of light and space are white walls and concrete flooring. The house contains a mix of both modern 20th-century classic pieces, such as a pair of black leather Mies Van der Rohe footstools and a Bertoia Diamond chair ("Classic seating has always been a particular passion of mine," says Urko), and vintage finds: reclaimed polished marble work surfaces and splashbacks in the kitchen, and a Victorian claw-footed, cast-iron tub in the master bathroom. Original features in the building – from brickwork to shutters at the windows – have been left intact wherever possible. Butterflies are a motif in this home, with a delicate wrought-iron butterfly window by Juan Calcarami in the bathroom, and Celina's twisted butterfly suspended from the ceiling downstairs. Urko's black and white photographs adorn the walls. "This place really is our refuge as well as where we create," he says, "and I feel fortunate in having such a magical environment in which I'm able to do both."

# This is an airy, light-filled refuge

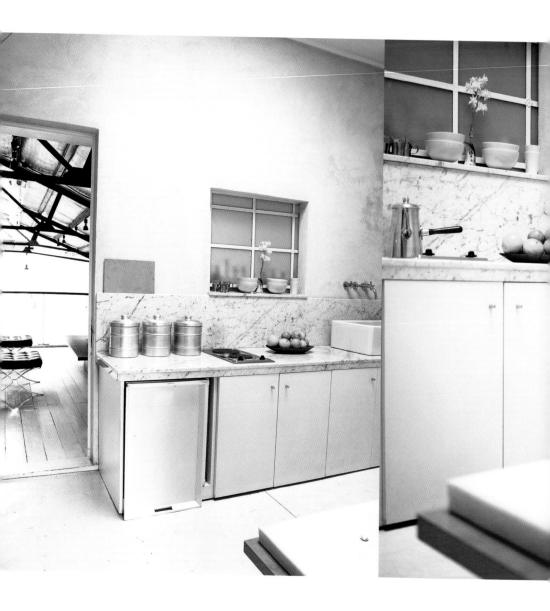